P9-CAD-709

Happy "44th"
Birthday, Carlene

Love—
M. J.

Aug. 19, 1989

A Gathering Of Wishes

A Selection Of
Writings On Celebrations

By Flavia Weedn

Roserich Designs, Ltd.
Carpinteria, California

Library of Congress Cataloging in Publication Data

A GATHERING OF WISHES
Printed in Hong Kong
ISBN 0-913289-34-5

This book
is a gift book of
wishes and celebrations.
It is intended
to be kept to remind us
of the joys in our lives...
or to be given
as a gift to someone
to embrace a time
of celebration.

Flavia

A
gathering
of wishes
that
your wish
comes true.

◆ ◆ ◆

Each
of us
is a part
of all
that
surrounds us...

. . . and
every joy
we feel
is
a celebration
of life.

◆ ◆ ◆

I
wish
you
time
for
simple
joys.

◆ ◆ ◆

*Surely
a star
danced in
Heaven
on the day
you were
born.*

◆ ◆ ◆

I
wish you
winter
sparklers,
summer
snowflakes...

...and
rainbow
rings
around
the
moon.

◆ ◆ ◆

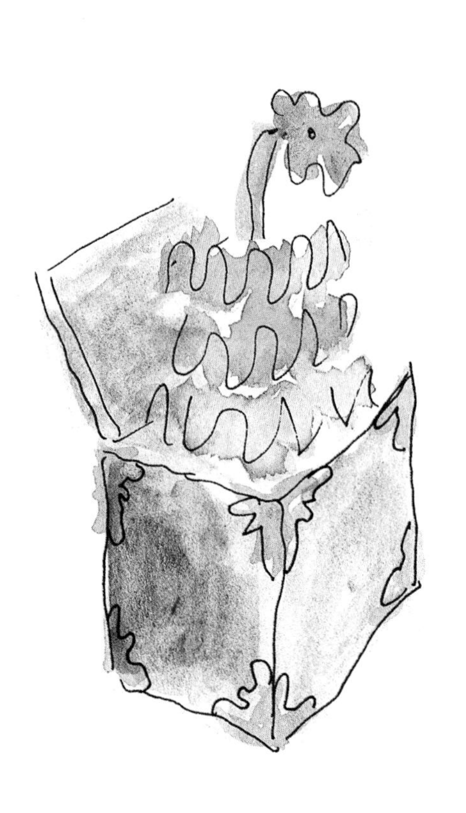

Wishing
you
the wonder
of an
unforgettable
day.

◆ ◆ ◆

In
every
ordinary
day,
there's
a
handful
of miracles.

◆ ◆ ◆

I
wish
you
love
to hold
when
you feel
empty...

*...and
a hand
to hold
when
you're
afraid.*

◆ ◆ ◆

Those
who
reach
touch
the
stars.

◆ ◆ ◆

All
it took
to get
there
was a
lucky
star...

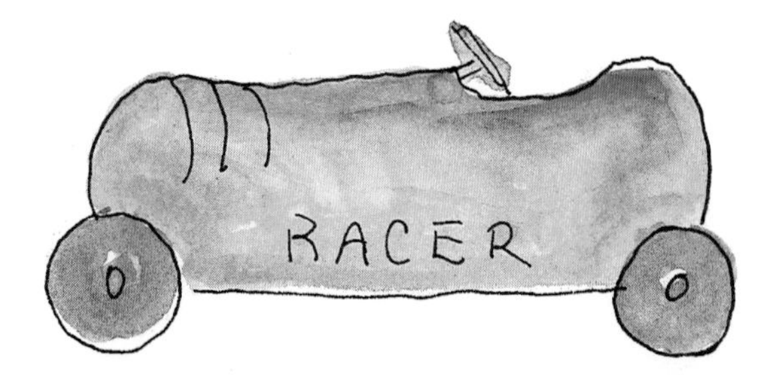

...a
handful
of dreams...
and
lots
of
hard work.

◆ ◆ ◆

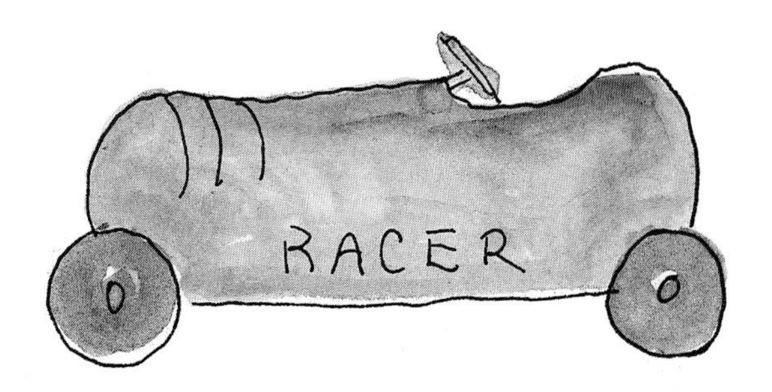

Wishing
you
a time
of dreams
and surprises
and
ice-cream
colored
days.

◆ ◆ ◆

May
the special
moments
of today
bring
you special
memories.

◆ ◆ ◆

If
I could
wrap love
in
a ribbon...

...it would
be
my gift
to
you.

◆ ◆ ◆

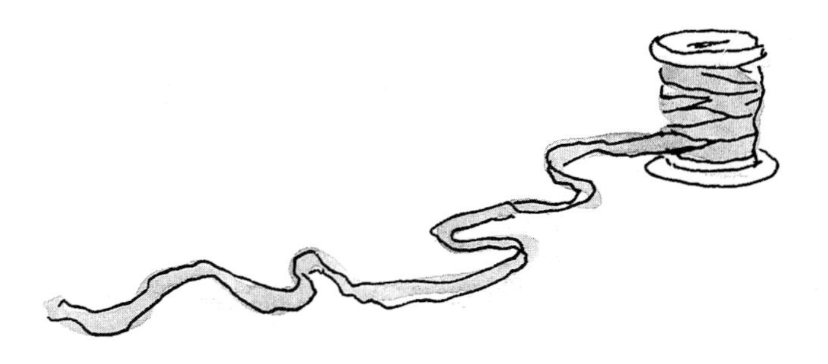

Life
is the
greatest
show
on Earth.
Embrace it.

◆ ◆ ◆

With
trumpets
and
fanfare,
I
wish you
a
magical
day.

◆ ◆ ◆

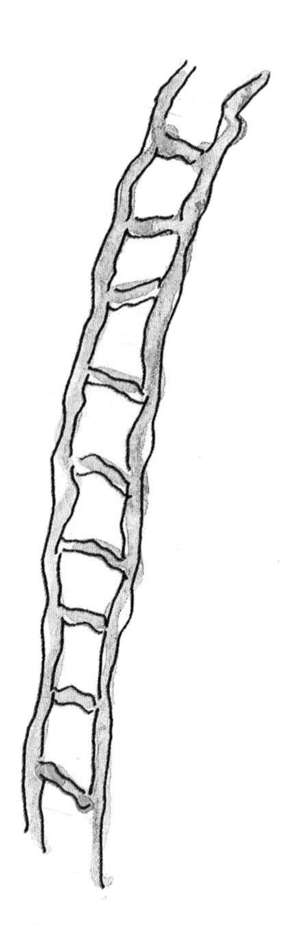

Let
your
eyes
stay
filled
with
stars…

...and
your heart,
with
glimpses
of dreams
yet to come.

◆ ◆ ◆

Once
upon a time
an angel said,
"The secret
of life
is enjoying
the passing
of time."

◆ ◆ ◆

Beautiful
things
happen
because
of
beautiful
people.

◆ ◆ ◆

What
each
of us
becomes,
is fashioned...

...from
the
stardust
of our
dreams.

◆ ◆ ◆

Life
is
fragile.
Be happy.

◆ ◆ ◆

The
greatest
joys
are
celebrations
of the
heart.

◆ ◆ ◆

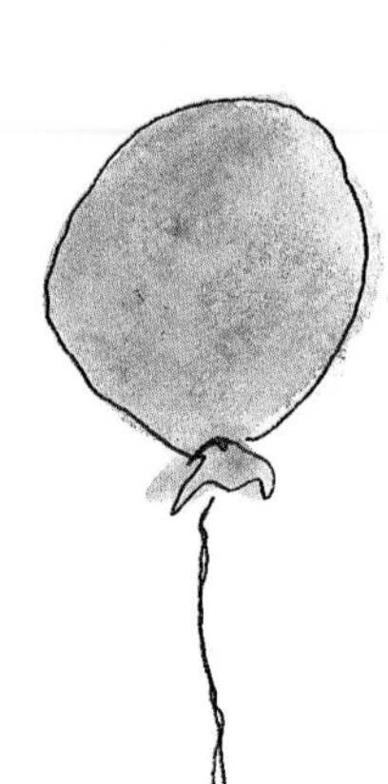

Our wishes
are the
magic
in our
minds...

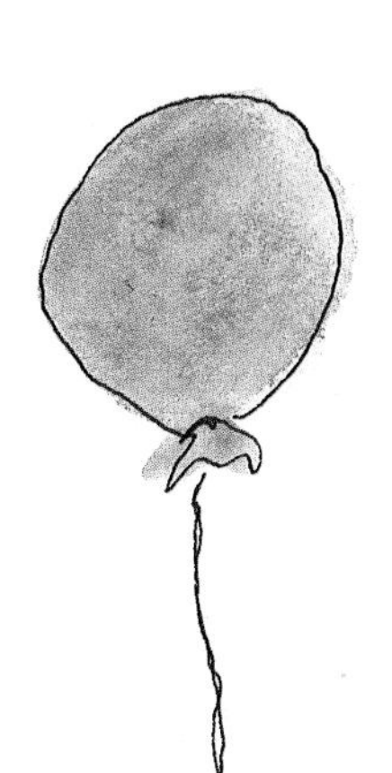

...that
cause
wonderful
things
to happen.

◆ ◆ ◆

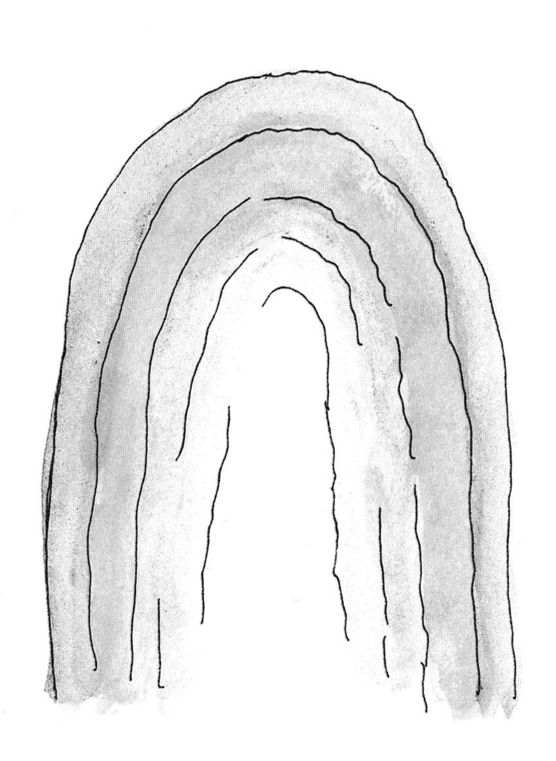

I
wish
you
a
rainbow,
and
a
handful
of
stars.

◆ ◆ ◆

Today
is
free
and
it's
yours.

◆ ◆ ◆

You
matter
in my
life.

Thanks
for
being
born.

◆ ◆ ◆

DREAMS

Wishing
you
health,
friendship
and
the pursuit
of
your dreams.

◆ ◆ ◆

Each year
in our lives
brings
its own
pleasures
and
sings
its own
songs.

◆ ◆ ◆

A
PARADE

It's
a
time
for
parades,
banners
and
jubilations.

◆ ◆ ◆

Anniversaries
are the
memories
our hearts
hold dear.

◆ ◆ ◆

May
your dreams
ride
on the wings
of
angels...

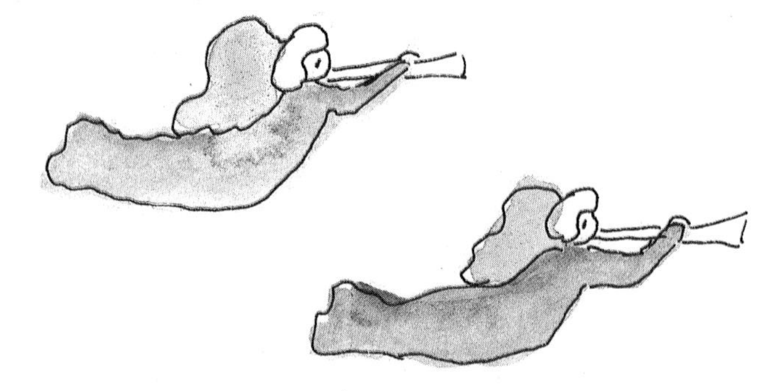

...and find their way to the skies.

◆ ◆ ◆

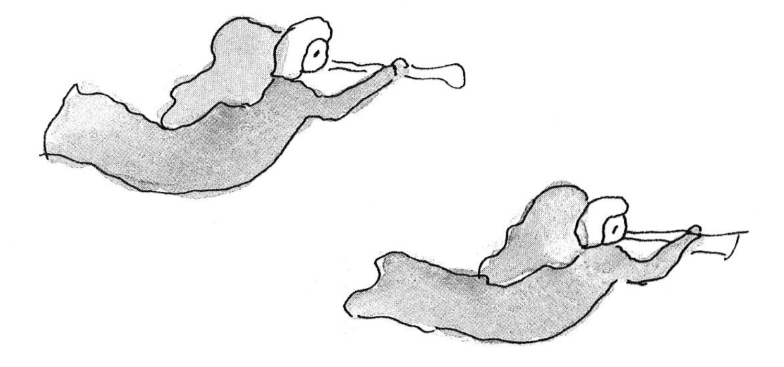

Wishing
you
all things
good
and
wonderful.

◆ ◆ ◆

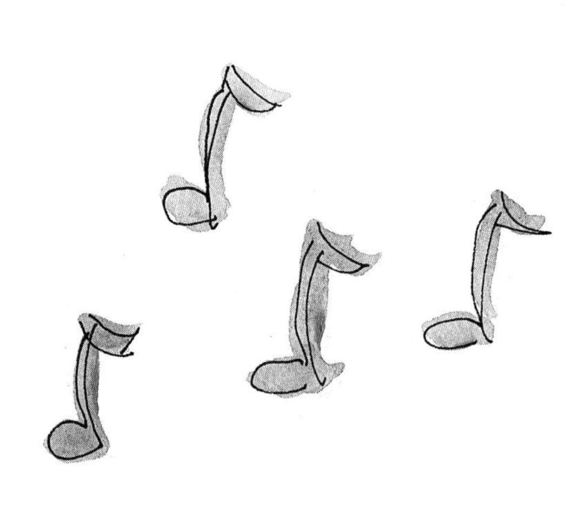

Life
is the music
that dances
through
our days,
our nights
and our
years.

◆ ◆ ◆

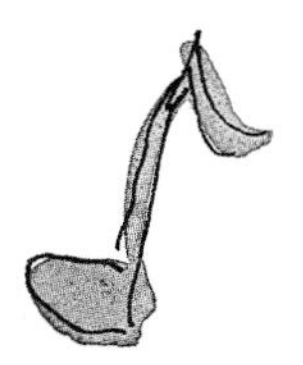 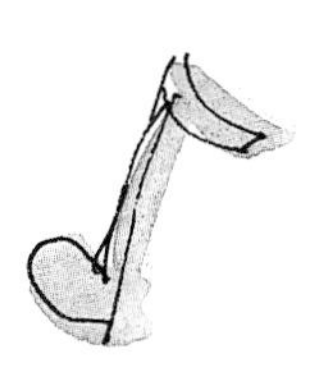 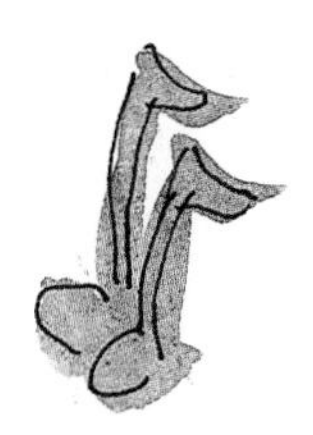

The
music
of life
is
different
to each
of us...

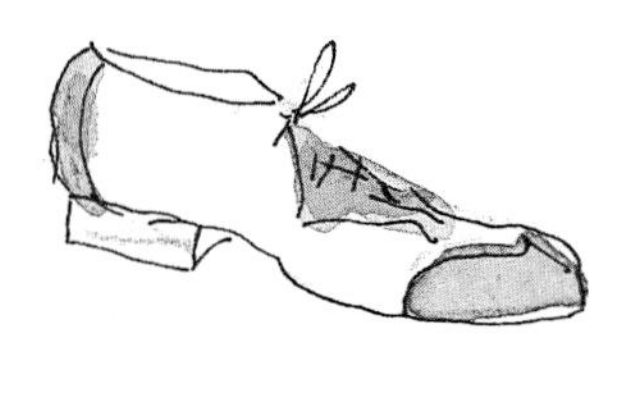

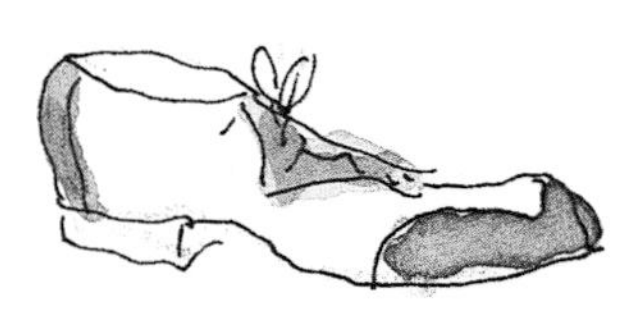

...but
how
beautiful
the
dance.

◆ ◆ ◆

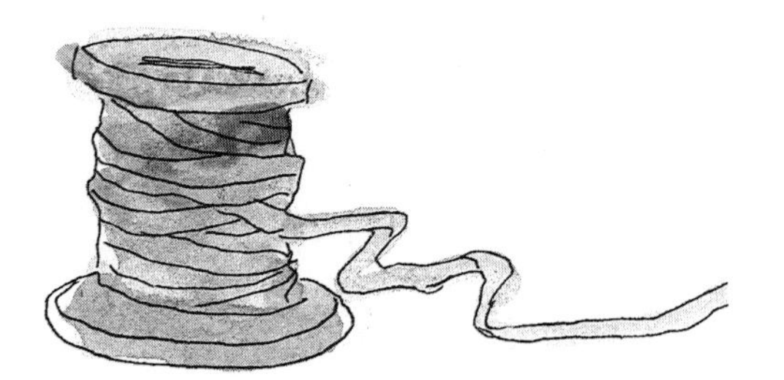

Every
celebration
is
a gift
from time.

◆ ◆ ◆

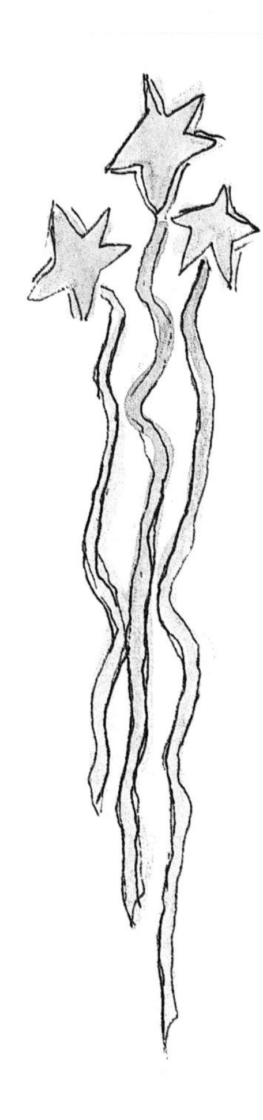

Never
be
afraid
to
dance
with
the
stars.

The
sky
is
made
of
music.

◆ ◆ ◆

The
truest
joy
of life
is the
ability
to love.

◆ ◆ ◆

May you
always
share love
and
laughter
with those
you love.

◆ ◆ ◆

Life
is a miracle,
and the right
to live
is a gift.
It's wrapped
in a ribbon
woven with dreams...

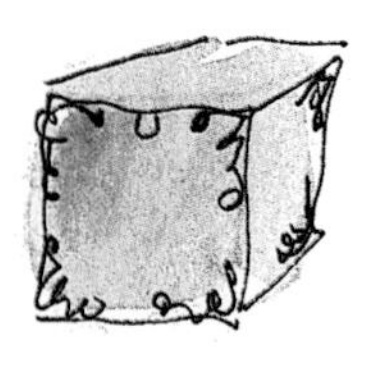
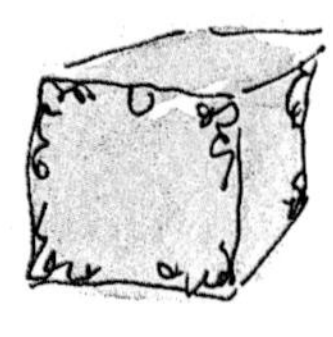

...and whether
you are very young
or very old,
life is filled
with wonder
and
surprises.

◆ ◆ ◆

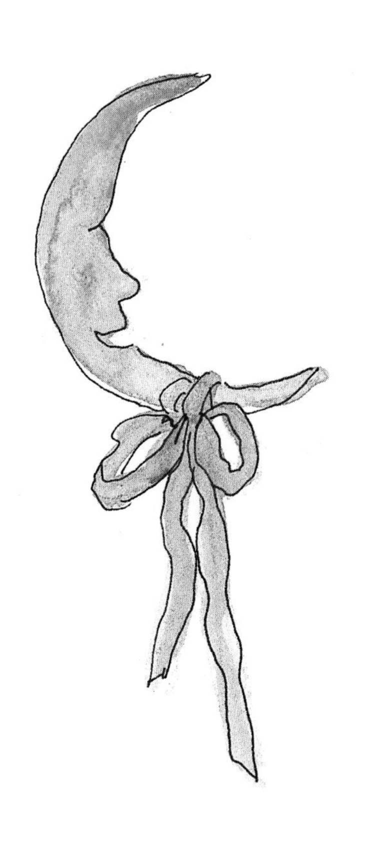

Today
is
unique.
Do something
wonderful
with it…
for it
will never
come again.

◆ ◆ ◆

The End

Flavia Weedn makes her home in Santa Barbara, California with her husband Jack and a big white cat named Charlie. She enjoys her family, her work, and the simple things in life.

Flavia has been painting and writing professionally for over 25 years but her work of late is truly her finest. Being a writer as well as an illustrator puts incredible demands on her time, however the endless deadlines never seem to scatter her. Painting and writing are Flavia's private passions, and she eagerly retreats daily into her octagonal studio, vintage 1940. French windows look out upon an acre of trees and a meadow overlooking the ocean. This brings her pleasure and allows her to gather her thoughts calmly while she absorbs the brilliance of this area she has chosen for her home; her beloved Santa Barbara.

When asked what her work represents she says quietly, "The incredibility of life that I feel; the beauty I see in ordinary moments and the need for people to express themselves honestly. In short, I try to bring hope to the human spirit."

Other Flavia titles include Wrapped In A Ribbon, Softly In Silver Sandals, Moments Shared, To Walk In Stardust and With Each Remembrance. Each is available through Roserich Designs, Ltd., PO Box 5003, Carpinteria, CA 93013-5003.

If you wish to know more about Flavia, please write to:
The Flavia Collectors Club, PO Box 5003, Carpinteria, CA 93013